SUMMARY
of Matthew Dixon and Brent Adamson's
THE CHALLENGER SALE

Taking Control of the Customer Conversation

by SUMOREADS

TABLE OF CONTENTS

EXECUTIVE SUMMARY

In their book *The Challenger Sale: Taking Control of the Customer Conversation*, Mathew Dixon and Brent Adamson argue for a new sales approach that bundles products and unique business insights to create broader value for the customer. The challenger sales rep—who has a keen understanding of business and industry and who uses this knowledge to push customers to think differently about their operations—epitomizes this approach.

Dixon and Adamson contend that in today's complex sales environment, B2B sales are harder to close because customers are unsure of their needs and more risk averse than ever before. Many sales reps, including the popular relationship builders, are struggling to stay afloat because customers want solutions, not just convenience. Challenger sales reps excel in this environment because they are trusted problem solvers: they teach customers new ways to save or make money, tailor their pitch to resonate with the objectives of the customer, and take control of the sales process.

Challengers differ from the other four categories of sales reps because they are different—they are assertive and memorable, and they lead *to* the solution, not *with* the solution, as is the norm in conventional feature-benefit selling.

Dixon and Adamson call on organizations working in complex sales environments to train and coach sales reps to be challengers and to set up organizational capabilities that make the challenger sale repeatable and scalable.

Key Takeaway: Go beyond solution selling to survive changing sales dynamics.

Conventional sales tactics are becoming ineffective in a complex sales environment. Products and services are becoming more complex and less differentiated, and B2B customers are considering purchase decisions with more vigilance. Customers are looking for supportive suppliers; suppliers who will address their perceived risks, customize their solutions at no extra cost, and offer maximum value on a purchase the way a third-party consultant would.

The recession that followed the 2008/09 financial crisis especially made B2B selling a near-impossible task. Yet, as sales plummeted, a few sales reps maintained their sales at record highs. They met their quotas because they shifted their focus from products to solutions. They bundled their products with unique insights to meet broader customer needs sustainably and in a way competitors could not replicate.

Key Takeaway: There are five distinct profiles of sales reps.

Depending on their attitudes, knowledge, skills, and the way they interact with customers, B2B sales reps fit in one of five distinct profiles:

The hard workers are self-motivated and enthusiastic. They make all-out efforts, persevere, and continuously seek feedback and growth.

The relationship builders' primary focus is building and nurturing relationships. They make themselves accessible to customers and are eager to meet their needs.

The lone wolves take on a self-assured attitude. They follow their instincts more than the rules. In this way, they are difficult to control.

The reactive problem solvers focus on post-sale customer service. They pay more attention to solving customer problems and ensuring their satisfaction than to generating new sales.

The challengers leverage their in-depth knowledge of the customers' business to push their customers to take on a different perspective and compete more effectively. They bring new insights not just to their customers, but to their managers, as well.

Key Takeaway: Challenger reps are effective because they teach, tailor, and take control.

Challenger sales reps make up about 40 percent of the high performers in leading sales teams. Only 7 percent of relationship builders are star performers.

Challengers outperform core performers because their unique insights into the value drivers of their customers' businesses enable them to tailor their message to resonate with the customer. They teach their customers to differentiate their business and they take control of negotiations and the sales process.

Relationship builders underperform the other categories of sales reps because they focus on getting along with customers and easing them into a comfort zone. In a complex sales environment, offering comfort can only take you so far. Challengers, on the other hand, use constructive tension to push customers out of their comfort zone. They offer value where relationship builders offer convenience.

Challengers offer the most value in complex sales models that call for solutions selling. In ordinary, transactional sales where success depends on volume sold, hard workers win the day.

Key Takeaway: Adopting the Challenger Model is an organization-wide, long-term investment.

Implementing the Challenger Model is a process that takes time—usually a few years to get to full adoption. Organizations have to invest in developing their capabilities, not just the skills of their sales reps, to support their teams and ensure that the content they deliver is scalable, repeatable, and offers uniform value.

To implement the Challenger Model successfully, organizations have to invest in sales reps skills and organizational capabilities concurrently. They have to invest in training and follow it up with coaching, and they have to research insights and find the right sales managers,

Key Takeaway: The purchase experience wins more loyalty than the quality of brand, product, and service delivery combined.

A company's brand and product and service delivery only account for about 38 percent of customer loyalty. Low value to price ratio only wins about 9 percent of customer loyalty. The sales experience, on the other hand, contributes to more than 50 percent of customer loyalty. Customers are more likely to keep buying more from a supplier and recommending its services if the supplier offers valuable insights about the market, offers ongoing advice on alternatives and new issues, helps the customer avoid potential risks, and enjoys widespread support in the customer's organization. Customers are loyal to suppliers who engage them in conversations they would ordinarily pay for.

"Customer loyalty is much less about what you sell and much more about how you sell. The best companies don't win through the quality of the products they sell, but through the quality of the insight they deliver as part of the sale itself" (Kindle Locations 907-908).

Key Takeaway: Star sales reps go beyond discovering needs; they teach new insights.

Conventional wisdom has it that sales are driven by understanding customer needs and matching products or services to these needs. This perception assumes that customers know what they need.

Challengers know that customers don't always know what they need. They use their understanding of their customer's business to tell them what they need.

In a complex sales environment, customers are looking for sales reps who will help them cut costs, increase revenue, find new opportunities, and mitigate risks. They are looking for suppliers who understand their needs better than they do and offer new insights to improve their businesses.

Key Takeaway: Focus on commercial teaching to increase conversion.

New insights don't win business by themselves. If you talk about what you can't offer, or what you can't offer well, what you're offering your customer is free consultation.

Sales reps have to teach valuable insights in a way that actually leads to sales. To do this, they have to tie the insights they emphasize as valuable to what they offer better than the competition. Organizations have to understand and agree on their unique value proposition so sales rep know how to structure their message.

The insights sales reps offer have to challenge, not merely validate, what customers think about their business. Challengers get customers curious and interested by highlighting the trends they overlooked, the burgeoning risks they missed, and anything that they may not have considered before. They speed up action by nudging customers to calculate the savings or other benefits they are missing out on when they don't take up the opportunity they offer.

Organizations are at the heart of everything that makes the Challenger Model repeatable and scalable. They have to group customers with similar needs or behaviors, craft insights that will tap into these needs, and equip sales reps with these insights and challenger skills. Organizations prepare the conversations that the sales reps will have with the customers.

Key Takeaway: Teach with stories, not spreadsheets, to engage the customer.

A good teaching pitch tells a compelling story that engages both the rational and emotional minds of the customer. There are six steps to a winning pitch. The last thing the sales rep mentions is the solution because the customer cares more about his problems than what the rep is selling.

1. Introduce the challenge. After the introductions, talk about the challenges facing the customer's industry and business (such as rising costs) and ask for a reaction. The objective is to demonstrate empathy and build credibility.

2. Reframe the challenge. Once the customer acknowledges the challenges you mentioned, link those challenges to a bigger challenge (such as an overlooked reason for rising costs) or opportunity the customer hasn't anticipated. The reaction you are going for is surprise, not agreement.

3. Argue for the reframe. Use the data you have to demonstrate to the customer the cost of overlooking the problem or opportunity you mentioned. Make a compelling case that elicits fear, uncertainty, and doubt.

4. Make it personal. Describe a scenario familiar to the customer—perhaps a scenario where similar companies are dealing with undesirable outcomes that result from behaviors typical to the industry. The objective is to get the customer to realize they are not different; the problem is as real for them as it is for everyone else.

5. Propose a solution. Review what the customer will need and how he would mitigate the problem or take advantage of the opportunity. The customer has to embrace the solution before he buys into yours.

6. Offer your solution. Sell the customer on your unique capabilities to show how you can deliver a tailored solution better than the competition.

"...in your customers' eyes, your primary value as a supplier is your ability to teach them something, not to sell them something. In the teaching world, the pitch isn't about the supplier at all. It's about the customer" (Kindle Locations 1217-1219).

Key Takeaway: Build your teaching pitch from the end to fit your unique value proposition.

When you build your pitch, focus on the parts of your solution customers underappreciate or are unaware of. That's how you challenge or teach them something new. Customers are likely aware of the core strengths of your solution. Find what you do best—why your customers buy from you—and build on that.

For your teaching pitch to be effective, it must focus on big, risky ideas that are difficult for the customer to implement. It must also offer an innovative approach for solving the customer's problem.

Remove common buzzwords such as "leader," "best," "unique," "solution," and "innovative" from your pitch. They make you sound like every other player in the market. If you can't structure your pitch around a unique insight, no wording will make your offer unique.

Key Takeaway: Secure the support of organizational stakeholders to win consensus sales.

Complex products have anticipated the age of consensus purchases. Swelling product features and alternatives, coupled with the recent economic downturn, have reduced the risk tolerance of procurement decision makers. Senior executives and procurement officers are now, more than ever, consulting their teams before making purchase decisions.

For most senior executives, the support a supplier has within the organization is the most important driver of loyalty, followed only by the ease and speed of the selling experience. Securing the backing of organizational influencers is the indirect path to the decision maker's support and loyalty.

Both influencers and decision makers find it easy to establish rapport with sales reps who demonstrate a high level of professionalism and offer unique insights that enable them to avoid pitfalls, increase efficiency, and ease their work. The challenger rep knows customer stakeholders influence the purchase decision more than he does, so he goes to them with his insights first.

Key Takeaway: Tailor sales messages to individual stakeholders to create resonance.

Tailored messages are messages that give the customer a better understanding of their company and industry. When you create a sales message, consider industry trends and regulatory changes and how they affect the customer's value drivers. Consider the risks your customers face and the results they want to achieve.

Through the marketing department, the organization can find out what each group of customer stakeholders is responsible for, what it wants to accomplish, and what it is concerned about, and arm sales reps with these insights.

It's not necessary to interview every marketing or information officer in the industry; the concerns of a few people in similar companies and roles reflect the concerns of the entire industry. The key is to find what stakeholders are focused on and the activities or levers that can drive business outcomes in these areas.

With these insights, the organization creates conversational guidelines that ease the challenger sale. It prints customer concerns, areas of focus and desired outcomes, as well as the potential sources of value, on cards that sales rep take with them to stakeholders. On the same cards, it matches organizational capabilities with the desired outcomes of each

14

group of stakeholders. It also crafts outcome statements that cover the activity or behavior to be improved, the means to achieve desired outcomes, the metric to be used, and the magnitude of the expected change.

The goal is to create a template for a conversation about the concerns of the customer, the specific outcomes that need to be achieved, and the solutions the supplier offers. The sales rep should address stakeholders as if they were the decision makers to get a buy-in that will influence the decision of the executive.

Key Takeaway: Take control of the sales process to beat customer skepticism.

Customers are bound to push back at the sales rep, regardless of the value of his solution. They will argue they are different, that they don't need the solution. Challengers take control of the sales process to convince the customer of the familiarity and urgency of the problem they face.

Challengers take control of the entire sales process—from pushing customers to think differently about their challenges to leading the negotiations. They are comfortable pushing customers and walking away from unfavorable deals because they know the value they offer with their unique insights.

Unlike regular sales reps, challengers don't let the customer lead the sales process. Instead of asking the customer how the sale will proceed, the challenger draws from experience or research to teach the customer about the process—

including who will be involved and how the solution will be implemented.

Taking control doesn't mean being aggressive. Challengers are assertive; they aim for the middle ground between being passive and aggressive. They are direct, clear about their goals, and respect their boundaries and those of their customers.

Key Takeaway: Plan in advance to negotiate with confidence.

Create a template that includes your strengths and weaknesses relative to those of the customer. Include concessions you will be willing to offer and the concessions you will ask the customer to make. Put a value on each of these concessions. This way, you are clear beforehand about the value of your proposition and the value you are willing to exchange. Include the difficult questions and objections you anticipate from the customer.

Key Takeaway: Create constructive tension to take control of negotiation.

Most sales reps cave in to customer demands prematurely because they would rather not endure the ambiguity and tension that comes with being assertive.

Taking control of the negotiation process is a delicate balance that begins with acknowledging the demands or objections of the customer and offering to address them after exploring his needs. Deferring customer demands creates tension that is best managed by shifting the attention of the customer to other solution features important to him, other than price or other subject of protest. The sales rep only comes back to the price when the customer has fully understood how the solution will help him create value and achieve specific business outcomes.

When the customer understands the value, the sales rep asks for the rationale of the customer's demand. It's important that the sales rep start with a meaningful concession and reduce the value of subsequent concessions as he proceeds. The objective is to make the customer feel he won, not cheated.

Challengers create tension in the sales process by making robust requests. When the customer buys into the solution, they ask for speedy commitment to implement it.

Key Takeaway: Secure the buy-in of frontline sales managers to execute the Challenger Sales Model.

The successful execution of the Challenger Sales Model hinges not just on the involvement but on the effectiveness of frontline sales managers.

The people who make star sales managers have three key qualities: they are reliable, they have integrity, and they listen. More than that, they are good at selling, coaching, allocating resources, and coming up with innovative ways to structure offers and solve deal-related problems.

When coaching, sales managers should focus on behaviors, not outcomes, and customize coaching sessions to individual sales reps.

Key Takeaway: Emphasize sales innovation to find better ways to secure deals.

Of all the sales-related attributes a sales manager could possess, sales innovation is the single biggest predictor of excellence. This finding makes sense considering the modern day's complex sales environment. Unlike coaching, which steers sales reps to known behaviors, innovating is about helping them navigate the unknown.

Sales managers are innovative if they excel in three activities: investigate obstacles to new sales from the information provided by sales reps, create new ways to position solutions, and share best practices with their sales reps and other organizational members.

"Sales success today is much less about getting better at what you already know and much more about creating an ability to tackle what you don't know" (Kindle Locations 2464-2465).

Sales innovation also calls on managers to shift from "narrowing" thinking to "opening" thinking. In the typical narrowing thinking, sales managers look for the best solution in a basket of options. In opening thinking, the focus is on generating more options to pursue. Opening thinking is about looking beyond practical ideas, ideas that have worked in the past, and the first ideas that come to mind. It is about finding new ways to substitute, combine, and magnify the features of solutions.

EDITORIAL REVIEW

At a time when B2B sales are becoming harder to close, a few stellar performers are still meeting—and often exceeding—their quotas. In *The Challenger Sale*, Dixon and Adamson dig into years of research to illustrate how sales reps differ in their behaviors, skills, and approaches, and how the top performers successfully navigate a complex sales environment. The authors argue that star sales reps bring more than exceptional products or services to the table; they offer invaluable insights and customized solutions that match their customers' objectives. They don't discover needs; they teach customers what they need and link the solutions they propose to what they do best.

After studying more than 6,000 sales reps in different industries across the globe, Dixon and Adamson draw five distinct categories of sales reps: the hard worker, the relationship builder, the lone wolf, the problem solver, and the challenger. They offer a brief overview of each of these profiles and dedicate the bulk of the book to uncovering the learnable approach that gives challengers an edge over the other types of sales reps.

In not so uncertain words, Dixon and Adamson predict the death of solution selling and envisage a future with jobless relationship builders and thriving Challengers. This prediction, which their research supports, has drawn the ire of thought leaders who lament over the authors' oversimplification of solution selling. The authors only concede briefly that hard workers can outperform challengers in non-complex sales environments.

To a large extent, *The Challenger Sale* builds on the solution selling that it so much disparages. The approach is different—with solution sellers focusing on existing needs and challengers on undiscovered needs—but the objective in both models is to uncover and address unmet customer needs. When it comes to the pitch, challengers rely as much on story telling as solution sellers do.

The authors' saving grace is the compelling findings from their research, their success implementing the Challenger Sales Model—part of which they cover in a few case studies—and, perhaps, the commendation by professor Neil Rackham, the solutions-leaning author of SPIN selling, in the foreword.

Towards the end, the authors offer practical guidelines for implementing the Challenger Sales Model. They explore the concerns of implementers—which they have gathered from years of guiding organizations toward the Challenger Sales Model—and advise them to consider piloting the model before making a full organizational launch.

The authors also explore applications of the model beyond sales—in internal processes such as IT and marketing—to make *The Challenger Sale* a comprehensive guide for not just sales reps, but senior executives and leaders of functional teams. Non-sales employees, Dixon and Adamson contend, can use the Challenger Sales Model to deliver compelling business insights to top management (internal customers) and become indispensable organizational partners.

ABOUT THE AUTHORS

Mathew Dixon is the Global Head of Sales Effectiveness Solutions at Korn Ferry Hay Group and a management executive at CEB. He has coauthored three business books, including his bestseller with Adamson, *The Challenger Customer*, and has been published numerous times in the Harvard Business Review.

Brent Adamson is the Principal Executive Advisor at CEB and a sought-after facilitator of executive-level discussions on sales and marketing. Adamson is also a frequent contributor of the Harvard Business Review and Bloomberg BusinessWeek.

THE END

If you enjoyed this summary, please leave an honest review on Amazon.com…it'd mean a lot to us.

If you haven't already, we encourage you to purchase a copy of the original book.

by **SUMO**READS

Made in the USA
San Bernardino, CA
05 June 2018